A Dress for Kathleen

Heather Richardson

Story Mach\ne

A Dress for Kathleen, copyright © Heather Richardson, 2023

Print ISBN: 9781912665297
Ebook ISBN: 9781912665303
Published by Story Machine
130 Silver Road, Norwich, NR3 4TG;
www.storymachines.co.uk

Heather Richardson has asserted her right under Section 77 of the Copyright, Designs and Patents Act 1988 to be identified as the author of this work.

All rights reserved. No part of this publication may be reproduced, stored in a retrieval system, or transmitted in any form or by any means, graphic, electronic, recorded, mechanical, or otherwise, without the prior written permission of the publisher or copyright holder.

This publication is sold subject to the condition that it shall not, by way of trade or otherwise, be lent, re-sold, hired out or otherwise circulated without the publisher's prior consent in any form of binding or cover other than that in which it is published and without a similar condition including this condition being imposed on the subsequent purchaser.

Set in Garamond.

Printed and bound in the UK by Seacourt Ltd.

Story Machine is committed to planet positive publishing. Our world is better off for every single book we print.

Story Machine is committed to the environment.
This document is printed using processes that are:

100%
Net Carbon Negative

100%
Renewable Energy

100%
ISO14001

100%
eco-friendly simitri® toner

100%
Recyclable Stock

Zero% waste to landfill

Printed by **seacourt** – proud to be counted amongst the top environmental printers in the world

A Dress for Kathleen

Heather Richardson

In memory of my dad, Tom Hutchinson

Contents

Heaven is our Home 1
Kathleen 9
Webs 25
Thomas 33
Homeplace 49
Hannah 57
Dressmaking 71
Afterword 81

Heaven Is Our Home

Every family has shadow people, the ones who slipped out of the story too soon, leaving a blank space where they should have been. In my father's family that person was his sister Kathleen, who died in December 1939 at the age of fourteen. Cycling home from work on a Friday night, on a dark country road made darker by the wartime blackout, she didn't see a local farmer, Robert McCahon, making his own way home by foot. Perhaps she swerved at the last minute: he reported feeling something touch his right hand and then hearing a crash. The fall knocked her unconscious, and she was bleeding from a cut above her left eye. McCahon lifted her to the side of the road and went for help.

There was a little shop nearby at a junction of country roads known as the Cross Keys, and the shopkeeper, Lily Canning, had a car. She drove Kathleen to the nearest doctor some five miles away in the village of Swatragh, and he in turn took her to the infirmary in Magherafelt where she was admitted some time after midnight. She died in the early hours of Sunday morning without ever regaining consciousness.

I knew about Kathleen from visits to my grandparents at their home in the County Derry town of Kilrea. Not that she was talked about – not at all. But she was buried in the graveyard of St Patrick's Parish Church, just a short walk up the road from my grandparents' house. If our visits fell on a summer Sunday the Kilrea cousins would take my brother and me for a walk. The town had limited places of interest for us youngsters: a tiny play-park tucked away beside the primary school, a gnarled fairy thorn on Church Street, kept upright by rusted iron struts, and Kathleen's grave.

The plot was marked with a modest cross and surrounded by large white pebbles of the sort you might pick up on the beach at White Park Bay thirty-odd miles away on the north Antrim coast. Kathleen was buried beside her baby sister, Ruth. (Poor Ruth is hidden even further in the shadows than Kathleen. Born in 1930, the fourth of my grandparents' children, she lived only fourteen days. Her death certificate records the cause of death as 'congenital debility'. She was born weak, in other words, and in the days before the NHS and Special Care Baby Units the odds were against her.)

I was intrigued by death, as children often are. But I had little direct experience of it, being blessed with a full quartet of long-lived grandparents. Kathleen challenged my understanding of time and family. Could I call her my aunt when she had died twenty-five years before I was even born? Both my parents had a sprawling, fecund heritage where generations of women gave twenty or thirty years of their lives to pregnancy, birth and childrearing. Dad was one of eleven children, Mum one of eight. I found it impossible to conceptualise having a sibling who was decades older or younger than me. It was still more impossible to imagine what the death of a child might do to a family.

If you go to the churchyard in Kilrea now you'll not find the simple grave with the white stones around it. A wide new grave-surround was installed – polished black granite filled with quartz chips – after my grandparents died and were buried in the same plot. It's in a beautiful spot, as graves go, shaded by a venerable copper beech.

In the years since then the grave has filled up as Kathleen, Ruth and their parents were joined by two more of the children – Anna and Jack – both of whom managed the full span of years their sisters never saw. The black granite headstone has grown crowded with names. Engraved at its base, partly hidden by grave pots and arrangements of artificial flowers, are the words HEAVEN IS OUR HOME.

There was nothing remarkable about Kathleen's short life, but it has become for me a doorway into unexplored corners of my family's past and the world they inhabited. My father was only six years old when she died, but the memory of that bleak December remained seared in his memory, and in the collective memory of his family.

Kathleen was born in 1925, the second child of Thomas and Hannah Hutchinson. Her father had fought with the 36th Ulster Division in the First World War, and survived the carnage of the Somme. After the war he joined the police and served during the turbulent years before and after the partition of Ireland. Thomas was an intelligent but difficult man. His childhood was blighted by blinding headaches that forced him to abandon his schooling early on, and as an adult he was prone to resentments and fallings-out. No doubt his experiences of violence both as a soldier and a policeman contributed to his temperament.

It was during his time with the police that he married Hannah, a farmer's daughter, who was twelve years his junior. She had played her own part in the war effort in her early teens, working in the household of a veterinary surgeon and travelling with his family to the military training camp on Salisbury Plain where he attended to the army horses.

By the time Kathleen was born her father had settled into a job with the LMS railway company. The family lived in a railway 'gatehouse' in the townland of Drumagarner, just outside Kilrea. The gatehouse stood beside the train line that ran from Macfin Junction to Magherafelt. In 1939, at the age of fourteen, Kathleen left school and began work as a trainee typist in the offices of William Clark and Sons, a linen manufacturer in the village of Upperlands, six miles from the gatehouse. Every day, as summer turned into autumn and rumours of war became a reality, she made the journey to and from work on her bicycle.

Ideas for ways I might explore Kathleen's life emerged slowly. I tracked down her birth certificate and death certificate, but there was little in between except two photographs and my elderly dad's memories. I thought I knew more about my grandparents, Thomas and Hannah, but when I reflected about it more deeply I realised they were nearly as mysterious to me as Kathleen was. My father's life had taken him much further away from home than might be suggested by the forty miles between Kilrea and Belfast, where we lived. We visited his parents two or three times a year, and they were shy and silent in the presence of this son who'd gone to the big city and made good. All I really knew of them were fragmentary anecdotes that had been told and retold so many times they bore little imprint of the real experiences they described. But where knowledge runs out imagination takes over, and in re-imagining Kathleen I also re-imagined Thomas and Hannah. This book is a blend of fact and fiction, and the life stories of Kathleen, Thomas and Hannah are told through glimpses of their hidden lives.

*

Kathleen's death left a deep wound between her parents that I suspect never really healed. Tragedy casts a long shadow, but our lives are made up of light as well as darkness. I hope I have captured both in the words that follow.

Kathleen

8th January 1925 – 17th December 1939

Night-thoughts in the Gatehouse

There's a gun buried out in the moss. Daddy won't say where. He'd rather it was lost forever than hand it in.

The walls sweat in the winter.

The table is only big enough for three. We take turns to eat.

Daddy found an orphan fox cub. He gave it to the boys for a pet. They kept it in a cage. It wouldn't take the food they offered.

There's a girl at school is an only child. She says she has a bed to herself.

I like the night before washday best. The bolster case is soft with a week's worth of dreams.

Sometimes I think I hear a train coming. Daddy says it's just the rails talking in their sleep.

Train Times

The first train passes by just after eight, a sign for us to finish our breakfast and get on our way to school. We walk along the train track into Kilrea. At dinnertime I find a quiet spot in the schoolyard and listen for the whistle of the midday train from Magherafelt. I think of Daddy, at work on the line or in the station. I think of Mammy, raising her head from her housework to watch from the gatehouse window until the train passes.

After school we take the long way home. It's not safe to walk on the track then, with the afternoon train coming through.

The weeks when Daddy's on gatekeeping duty I go out to help him in the evenings. The late train in wintertime is my favourite. I love standing in the pitch-black cold, waiting for it to thunder out of the darkness, its chimney a cloud-maker, its wheels spitting sparks.

Seamstress

When I was wee I thought the Moores were special people. There was always someone walking up the lane towards their house, carrying a parcel. Mammy laughed when I told her. 'Not at all,' she said. 'They're bringing their coats to Tillie Moore. They're wanting them turned before winter.'

One day I watched Walter Tuppen pass by with a package wrapped in brown paper, and return again empty-handed. I ran up to the Moores'. Tillie was in the back room. 'Can I see how you do it?'

'You'll be here a while,' she said.

She was right. It was a slow business. She had a wee blade to unpick the stitches. First the lining came out. She hung it on the chair-back. It looked like the coat had shed its skin. And then she took the coat itself apart, seam-by-seam. I'd never thought about it before – how many parts there are to a coat.

'Take this bit to the window,' she said, handing me a sleeve. 'See the difference between inside and out.'

Even unpicked, the sleeve had the shape of Walter Tuppen's arm. The elbows were shiny and bagged with wear. Rippled creases where his elbow bent looked as if they'd been there forever. Inside, the fabric was darker, the nap lush.

'Quality worsted,' she said. 'It pays to buy the best you can. He'll get a good few years out of it yet.'

That winter I watched Walter Tuppen at church. His old coat like a new coat. All the wear and weariness hidden on the inside.

Disapprovals

Daddy has a long list of them: Baptists and Catholics, Presbyterians and Covenanters – dissenters of every stripe. Bosses and communists, sergeants and socialists. Land owners, home owners, horse owners. Long-nosed Bellingham and his holy-roller wife.

Wee Sister

Rosie Diamond sent us up the lane to Mrs Agnew. 'Stay away till you're sent for,' she said. The fields were ripe with barley. Mrs Agnew was milking the cow in the byre, singing hymns to the beast like she always did. *Low at his feet lay your burden of carefulness, high on his heart he will bear it for you.* I held Doreen's hand tight.

Lily Agnew took us to see the kitten. A wee black and white tomcat. He was still with his mammy. She hissed when we came too close.

It was near dark when we lit out for home. Mrs Agnew gave Bertie a pail of milk to take with us. 'Youse can bring the pail back the morrow,' she said.

Daddy was standing by the fire when we got home. Mammy was up and dressed. 'You've a new baby sister,' she said. We all rushed to peer in the crib.

'What's her name?' said Bertie. Mammy said she was called Ruth. She was ever so wee. Doreen looked like a giant beside her.

The baby was very quiet. She never cried. Mammy tried to nurse her. Doreen and I sang to her. *Low at his feet lay your burden of carefulness.* 'Don't let your daddy hear you singing that black-neb hymn,' Mammy said. Rosie Diamond came every day to help with her. 'I don't think she'll do,' she said. Then she saw that I was listening and sent me outside.

*

We were sent up the lane to watch the barley being harvested. Doreen started gurning and wanted to go home, but Bertie said we'd to stay out a while longer.

When we came back the baby was gone. The crib had been put away. Daddy didn't come home for tea. Mammy said he was away a message.

The Mercers' School

The classroom walls were hung with maps: the world; the Empire; Northern Ireland.

County Derry was folded in a drawer, like a tablecloth kept for best. 'Ordnance Survey', Miss Kidd announced, chalking the words on the board, then opened the map across her desk for us to see.

I thought it was like a quilt – the Derry line neat and sturdy as a double seam, running-stitch lanes, clustered French knots of trees.

It was Tillie Moore put that notion in my head. Said when she was first apprenticed to Lizzie O'Fee her head was full of stitching, night and day. She dreamt she was back in the classroom, cutting pattern pieces from those precious maps with her sharpest shears.

Imagine a dress made out of the world, she said.

Futures

Miss Kidd advised Coleraine Tech for shorthand and typing. Kate Turner was going too. We looked up the bus times. Kate said she would apply for the Civil Service when she was older. Find digs in Belfast. Go to dances.

Daddy said he'd spoke to someone at Clark's mill in Upperlands. They were looking a girl for the office. I could learn my typing as I worked. Bertie was already apprenticed there. The Clarks were ahead of the times. They had electricity in their houses. Bertie had been sent once to fit a light bulb in the dining room at Ardtara. Their children boated on the lake in the summertime, while the looms rattled and the beetling mill thundered.

Mammy said I should keep on with my learning a while more, but Daddy wouldn't listen. I told her I didn't mind. I liked the notion of working.

Once a week Daddy brings home a newspaper. Bertie and I read it when he's finished. There's a lot of talk about the war. Mammy and I made blackout blinds for the windows.

Sometimes I sit out by the train track, and think about all the places there are to go.

Journey

I can map the route from home to Upperlands by the smell, map the season to the month, to the week, nearly to the day, when someone says 'Remember last fair day?' or 'Mind the day when war was declared?' It isn't the date, or the sound of Mr Chamberlain's sombre voice on the wireless, or the mourning cattle roaring in the byres as their calves are sold in Bank Square – no, it's the smells. Cow parsley and hawthorn in the Maytime lane, or the turned earth and copper coins of pratie picking – nails black with soil – or the stink of the retting dam in high August. I put a colour on the smells – green, of course, mostly green, and yellow, and brown, the reds of winter, the slick grey of the road when the rain falls.

The Language of Linen

When I was at school I knew about flax flowers, and pulling lint when it was ready, and the retting dams and bleach greens. I knew each tiny flower would open in the morning and be withered by noon. Cycling from home to Upperlands these summer mornings I can see the blue hint of blossom in the flax fields.

The firm itself is told in colours. The brown room, the black dye house, the green race. The price lists are books of poetry. They teach me the language of linen. Holland in black, brown, pale and fancy colours. Military Buckram. Russian Crash. Sleeve Scrim. Collar Canvas. Union Dowlas. Huckaback. Unfinished.

The great ledgers on the high desks of the office are big as church bibles. Orders recorded in careful copperplate. I write names I've only seen in advertisements. Anderson & McCauley. The Athletic Stores. Arnott & Co. in Dublin. And others, more exotic. Auguste Dormeuil in London. Orders for damask napery and fine dress linen. And lately, black ARP cloth. 500 yards to Palace Barracks. 700 yards to the New Savoy Hotel. 900 yards to St Patrick's Barracks, Ballymena. At once. At once. At once.

Working Late
Friday 15th December, 1939

By the end of the day my fingers ache with the typing, especially my little fingers. They're tortured with stretching for the shift key on the monstrous Underwood typewriter. The older girls say my hands will toughen up to it eventually, but they've been saying that since August. There've been so many invoices to type I've only now noticed that the daylight's long ago faded outside the office window. 'Quick as you can, girls,' Mr Kenning says each time he emerges from his office. 'The sooner they're away the sooner the remittance comes in.' Then his phone rings and he'll scuttle back to his desk, ready to take another order. The last post is gone an hour ago, but still we work. 'I want the decks cleared before we finish,' Mr Kenning says. 'Next week will be even busier.'

It's the war, of course, and the blackout rules, that have the customers desperate. Yards and yards of 36-inch black ARP cloth needing dispatched at once the length and breadth of the country. It's always wanted at once. The military orders take priority, but there are all the smaller ones as well. Ladies in Belfast more accustomed to ordering finest dress linen are writing to Clarks for their blackout fabric.

At last Mr Kenning says we can finish up. He goes around the office checking the windows – not that they've been opened on a day like today – and opens the wee door of the stove to bank the embers.

'I suppose youse are off dancing the night, girls?' Lizzie Frazer jokes to us young ones as we button ourselves into our coats and burl scarves around our necks. It's a bleak, wet night, and all I want is to be home with a plate of food in front of me and a hot water bottle warming my bed. There's a Grand Carnival Dance happening in Kilrea Town Hall on Wednesday, but I won't be going. I'm too young for dances. Sometimes, when I walk into Kilrea with Lily and Kate on summer evenings, we see the older boys and girls dressed to the nines and knocking around outside the Mercers Arms or the Orange Hall until the music starts, or waiting for the bus to Ballymoney if one of the famous bands is playing there. We wonder how we might persuade our parents to let us go when we're older.

Notions of dancing are far from my mind tonight. Tomorrow I'll walk into Kilrea to buy Christmas treats for the wee ones, but for now my thoughts are on home. Most of the other girls walk on ahead as I get the carbide lamp on my bicycle lit. The glass is loose, and I have to twist it so that the black paper shade is in the right place. Daddy's warned me to make sure of it. The newspapers are full of cyclists being up before the judge for breaching the blackout laws.

The rain has stopped, thank goodness, but the lane from the office down to the main gate is heavy going, carpeted with wet leaves from the sycamores that line the way. As I get further along the sycamores are replaced by Scots fir. My lamp casts a tight circle of light on the ground just ahead of my front wheel and gives me little help in avoiding the pinecones that stud the lane. In daylight hours the lane is full of birdsong – the melodies of blackbirds and thrushes up near the office, and the stern cawing of the rooks from the dark thatch of the fir trees. Past 8 o'clock now on a December evening and there's no sound but the hiss of my cycle tyres and the whisper of the breeze in the treetops.

The path descends to the gate and I freewheel, saving my energy for the six-mile journey home. I don't stop at the gate, sweeping to the left onto the Kilrea Road. There are a few houses round about, but I can't see them in the absolute dark of the blackout. All I have is the trembling pool of light from the carbide lamp. As long as I can see it shining on the black gleam of wet tarmac in front of me I know I'm on the road and not in the ditch.

The first bit of the road out of Upperlands is level. Later on there'll be steep ups and downs as it ribbons its way over the hills, and then the last blissful downhill stretch towards Drumagarner and the gatehouse. Home.

I peddle harder as the road begins to rise. I've wrapped my muffler up over my mouth and nose and can smell the wool, warm and damp now with my breath. That's the great thing about cycling. As long as you're well happed up you'll be as snug as a bug. I crest the first hill and let the cycle freewheel as I come down the other side. I must be nearly at the Cross Keys by now.

Webs

The part of mid-Ulster where Kathleen grew up does not announce its beauty like other parts of Northern Ireland. It's a modest landscape under an epic sky. Viewed in passing from the motorway it's flat, but when I drive along the smaller roads connecting the villages and towns I notice the gentle rise and fall of the land, like the most sedate of rollercoasters. Travelling from Kilrea to Upperlands there are occasional glimpses of the Sperrin mountain range on the distant horizon. From this perspective the Sperrins are a low, broad mass. There are no showstopper peaks, nothing to distinguish one mountain from the next. These days the area is enjoyed by walkers, despoiled by quarry companies and even – in a spirit of misplaced optimism – mined for gold. In Kathleen's time it was *terra incognita* to most people: home to a few hardy hill-farmers, and the ideal spot to distil poitín – an illicit and blindingly strong liquor. When my grandfather was an A-Special in the early 1920s one of his jobs was to raid poitín stills. The only people who visited the Sperrins for leisure were well-to-do families like the Clarks – the owners of William Clark & Sons where Kathleen worked – who would load up their cars with picnics and shotguns for late-summer grouse-shooting excursions.

The Clark family had been involved in the linen business since the early 1700s, when John Clark, grandson of Scottish settlers, began to trade in the fabric in a small way. Over the next two hundred years business flourished as linen production became industrialised, and the family's fortunes blossomed likewise. The first buildings of the 'works' were built beside the narrow, fast moving Clady River where conditions were right for water-powered equipment. At that time there was no Upperlands village. The area surrounding the works was a sparsely populated townland, but over the decades that changed. Modest dwellings were built for the linen workers, and a series of splendid residences for the several branches of the Clark family.

Clark menfolk were expected to join the family business whether they liked it or not. 'Old' Harry Clark – who turned seventy the year after Kathleen died – had tried to break free by running away to sea when he was fifteen, only to be tracked down and retrieved by his father. His son, 'Young' Harry, took over the management of the works in 1925.

Upperlands is in some ways a hidden village. When I first drove through it I didn't realise it amounted to anything more than a few buildings scattered along the road. There's no church or pub, and the nearest primary school is over half a mile away on the road to Kilrea. The 1911 census showed a population of 358, and by 2011 this had increased to 561, but you'd never guess it unless you take the time to stop and explore.

My first visit is on a Sunday afternoon in the early summer. I park beside the Clady River, the golden-brown water drawing its colour from the peat bogs that blanket the land around here. The linen works is scattered around the village, a mix of old, new and derelict. There are two 18th-century stone buildings beside the car park – one has been restored as a visitor centre, and the other is a beetling house, where the woven fabric is pounded to give it the glossy appearance required for rich damask linen.

I cross the road from the visitor centre. The gateway

to William Clark & Sons opens into a lane shadowed on either side by Scots firs. Up above the rooks caw and squawk. As I walk further along the lane the pines give way to broadleaf trees, and the birdsong changes to the melodies and chirrups of blackbirds and robins. After a few minutes I come to a fork in the lane. The left hand path leads downhill to the modern works, where most of the company's production now takes place. Being a Sunday, it's closed up behind a locked gate. The right hand path leads up to a derelict building that once housed the office. This was where Kathleen worked. The date above the ruined door says 1929. This was an elegant Art Deco building in its time, painted powder blue, with the windowsills and slender pilasters picked out in air force blue. I tiptoe in, broken glass crunching under my feet. In Kathleen's day it must have been a modern and covetable workplace. The office then was equipped with a telephone, a dictograph and a typewriter, and the room was bright with electric and natural light. Orders were written by hand into huge ledgers that sat on high, sloped desks, and the wages books were similarly majestic in scale. Kathleen's death certificate gives her occupation as 'Typist' – a job that, for a girl from Kathleen's background, was quite prestigious. In the finely nuanced class structure of rural Northern Ireland, to be an office worker was considered superior to most other jobs available to young women. It was better than being a shop assistant, and a world above the female factory workers, regardless of how skilled they might be.

All that remains of the office interior now is a tiled floor and the shattered wooden framework that once formed a partition between the office itself and the equally derelict lapping room. The lapping room was where the finished linen was folded (or lapped) before going to market. Someone has spray-painted the statement *No Pope* on one of the walls.

It's hard to know what the working atmosphere in the office might have been. No doubt the manager, Mr Kenning, expected efficiency and deference, but it was almost certainly more relaxed than it had been a century earlier, when the rules for clerical staff forbade them from talking during business hours, or 'disporting themselves in raiment of bright colours'.

Something of that unforgiving spirit can be seen in Old Harry Clark's diaries. On an entry from 1935 recalling how a worker had accidently ruined fine dress linen worth £600, Old Harry notes, 'This man should never be employed in Upperlands again!' And in his account of the great lappers' strike of 1938 he notes, with satisfaction, 'We used this opportunity to reorganise the whole lapping room, and as a result we were able to do without a great many of the strikers, who never got back to work again.' Ironically, given those stern edicts against staff wearing bright clothes, much of the language of the linen industry is vibrant with colour and beauty. Old Harry's diaries are full of it. He refers to the brown room, the black dye house, the green race. I love the idea that the company can be described in colours. Old Harry also talks constantly of webs – how many were made, how many sold. A web is the whole piece of linen cloth as it comes off the loom, and in Old Harry's time would have been about 100 yards long.

In the days and weeks following the outbreak of war on 3rd September 1939, Old Harry makes careful note of events. Ships were sunk by the Germans and taxes were raised. Two of his sons joined the armed services. On September 16th he records that the son of a Clark's employee was killed when his ship, the HMS Courageous, was torpedoed. Reading the typescript of the diary in the Public Record Office in Belfast I turn to December, wondering what mention he'll make of Kathleen's death. He writes about the King returning to London after inspecting troops in France, and his son, Young Harry, returning from a trip to Scotland before Christmas. But there's nothing about Kathleen. I feel strangely hurt. Surely the death of a young employee in such tragic circumstances would have registered with him?

At least Old Harry's son and daughter-in-law, William Clark and his wife, sent a wreath to the funeral, as did the managers and office staff. At the inquest into Kathleen's death Mr Kenning 'spoke of the great loss caused by the death of the deceased, and expressed the sympathy of his directors with the bereaved parents'.

I've been back to Upperlands many times since that first visit. I love the walk up the lane to the old office building, the way the bird-music shifts from the rooks to the songbirds. Up beyond the old office is a series of dams, constructed to supply the works with power and water. In Kathleen's time these working dams doubled-up as a playground for the Clark children – boating in the summer, ice-skating when the water froze in the winter. These days, although still part of the company's property, there's a sense that the dams belong to the community. Teenage lads fish, and dog walkers enjoy the circuit around the man-made lakes. Local volunteers run the visitor centre as a labour of love. One of them is a descendant of Robert McCahon, the Ballygullib farmer who Kathleen swerved to avoid on that December night in 1939. In this part of the country land and family roots hold people fast. Like a different kind of web.

Thomas

1st May 1888 – 6th July 1984

White #1

Symptoms: First comes the flare of light behind his eyes. A drumbeat of blood so strong he thinks his head will burst. He is peeled. Raw. Even his hair hurts.

Triggers: The glare of paper on a bright day in the schoolroom. The snow, when it is pure and fresh fallen.

Diagnosis: The doctor murmurs to his mother. Congestion on the brain. What a voice that man has. Round and deep. Rolling like a sermon. *To be frank, Mrs Hutchinson, I doubt he'll live long enough to need much schooling.*

Cure: Anger and opportunity on the boil. He's drunk with it. Dark suits crowd him. His friend says something dirty about a girl they know. Laughter, high as a pig's squeal. Long tables. White paper. The pen in his hand. The ink. He concentrates, making his mark in swoops and curls. Cutting the whiteness with his name.

Portrait, 1916

Home leave, and his mother wants his portrait taken. Market day in Magherafelt. A photographer has set up shop in the parlour bar of Pat Murray's. A rattan chair, a side table, a sheet hung on the wall behind.

'Sit you here, sit you here,' the photographer says. A sleekit boy. Derry city accent. 'Turn towards me a wee bit. Let's see those sergeant's stripes.'

Sergeant. There's nothing like a bloodbath for advancement through the ranks. A door shuts: BANG. The wild red of burst flesh. A moment. A memory. But here, now. *No.* Not here. Not now. Just in his head. 'Take your cap off, would you? And put it on the table. Boys-a-dear, that's some head of curls.'

Waves, he thinks, not curls. Stubbornly choppy waves, only just held back with a hand's scoop of pomade.

'Lean your elbow on that there table. Cup your chin in your hand. Look over my shoulder, up and away. Think of your sweetheart –'

- *don't have a sweetheart –*

'– think of all those pretty French girls - '

- *their faces sour with suspicion and hunger –*

'Hold still,' the photographer says.

The flare. The flash. BANG. White. Red.

Wound

The work is no worse than hacking firs in the Garry Bog. Better soil. Good arable land. The birds sing in French. Sharp blue sky.

Next thing he's on his arse, the burn of shrapnel punched through his thigh. Like a cow's kick, both expected and unexpected. He knows at once this will not kill him.

The train rocks. Lullaby of pain.

Convalescence. The windows bright and high as a mill's. A red-haired Scottish nurse. The tang of her sweat when she attends to him. 'Let's see what that wound of yours is up to today,' she says with a wink, and draws the curtains round the bed.

The Land

He finds work for the corporation. One of the brethren put a word in. General labourer, piece work. Fixing roads. Clearing sheughs. Some days he's sent home. No pay. Work's scarce, and half the men maimed in body and soul.

The place has been festering since the war ended, like the black soup of a peat bog sweltering in the summer heat. Back in France, the trenches were always in flux. One day a landslip, the next day, shoring up. Things were lost and found and lost again, a muddy cycle of burial and exhumation.

The fields around the town are calm and green, but there's suspicion at the end of every laneway. The usual rumpuses on days when the blood runs hot. Rebellion rises and falls in waves. The Fenians never stop.

Let them go then, he decides. We neither want nor need them. Cut them off, those gangrenous green fields, before they poison ours. Let the squealing pigs run. And those ones who are penned in by land and enemies, painted into their corner, they can tip themselves into the sea or tip their cap to the King, for he's their King whether they like or not.

And yet, he knows that roads can be barricaded, but not the mountains. Not the rivers. Not the hearts. He knew a man used to hack out old trees that were buried in the Garry Bog. Deep down. Stone hard. He thinks of France. The trenches. And what he lost there.

Police Officer

He finds himself in uniform again. Two weeks' training and a six-month contract. They're called 'A'-Specials. Stationed in Cookstown barracks. His Webley loose in its holster. One of the other constables was at school with him. They say his brother connived to get the farm while he was away in France, and that's why he's so twisted. The Head Constable is a southerner. Fancies himself better than them.

They attend to the usual disorders. Turn over the Papists' houses in Orritor Street. There's talk of an IRA man in Annaghquin, but when they go there he can't be found. The sergeant sends them out into the moss, searching. They burn an outbuilding, to make their point.

Wife

Between contracts. On the light evenings him and the boys knock about the Diamond. Wall-leaning, toe-scuffing, kerb-kicking. Sharing smokes. Calling out to any girl that passed. *Hey girls, we're boys.* He feels too old for it, to be honest, but the house in Garden Street is cramped and crowded.

She comes walking by with her sisters. He knows the older girls from churchgoing, but he doesn't remember her. She'd have only been young when he went away to war. One of the boys says something cheeky. One of her sisters answers back. But she says nothing. Looks away down Broad Street. He can't tell what she's thinking.

Each time he meets her he tries to see something new. Her careful eyes. Her fine skin. One of the boys says something coarse, and he wants to batter him.

And then she's gone. Her sister says she has a job for the summer season, at a hotel up at Portstewart. He thinks to himself, *I can wait.*

Trades

Before the war he never knew the comfort of a steady wage. The army gave him that, though the price was high. Carry a gun for your living and you'll always be well paid.

It boils his blood to see lesser men than him get on, because he has no schooling. That sergeant in the Specials. The way he spoke to him. His wife was in a state when he told her he'd resigned. Went home to her mother with the baby. Her mother sent her back. He got work at the railway station, to pay the rent.

His duties now include: organizing his gang; filling in the time sheets; checking deliveries to Kilrea station; walking the line to check for damage; clearing dead beasts that were struck by the train; chastising those who let their beasts wander; snow duty; gate duty. He cultivates the earth on the embankment by the gatehouse. It's not his land, but who's to know? Grows praties, carrots, cabbages. Now and again he buys a pig and fattens it. He has money enough for a silver pocket-watch from Kelso's. His wife rears chickens and children. The weans go to school well fed. He wonders what they'll be fit for: Bertie – good with numbers, smart with his hands, his eyes set on the future; Kathleen – fond of her lessons; Doreen – fond of her own face in the mirror. And the younger ones. With them it's too soon to know.

When Bertie is apprenticed, he instructs him. Keep note of your hours. Check your pay. Question any shortfall. You need to watch those ones in the office. Don't let them make a fool of you.

Bertie's saving his money. Keeps a notebook. One of the boys in the Lodge told him he'd seen Bertie knocking around with Bellingham's daughter. He'll soon put a stop to that.

And Kathleen, then. There's respectable jobs for girls who can type. Fair pay, clean hands, and in out of the cold.

Nighttime
Friday 15th December, 1939

He sees it again, like a flare, like a flash, like a bang. Bertie bursting through the door with word of an accident. His face, eyes wide, gasping for breath. He goes over what Bertie said. A fall from her bicycle. Some farmer from Killygullib. He'll find him out.

Jimmy Begley has the use of a car. A nightmare of slow roads and darkness. Jimmy hunched over the wheel, smoking a Woodbine. Says it helps him to see.

Swatragh. More confusion. The sergeant raging at them from his bedroom window. Then the doctor's house. A civil man. Brings them in by the fire. A clock ticks on the mantelpiece, flanked by two china dogs. He finds a glass of whiskey in his hand, and Jimmy tugging his sleeve, telling him they have to go.

Infirmary

The corridor is full of shadows. He follows the orderly, who whistles as he walks. No tune. Just two notes, over and over, in time to his footsteps. He makes him wait outside the ward.

After a time he sits. His mouth is dry. He studies the floor. Counts the tiles on the walls.

He stands when the doctor comes to speak to him. Takes off his cap. The doctor talks like that young Captain he served under in France. He can't follow all he says. Some words stand out. *Fracture… concern… hope… prepare.*

They let him into the ward then. There are screens around her bed. The other patients cough and groan, restless in their sickness. Kathleen lies very still. He leans forward to hear her breathe. She is so pale. He speaks to her quietly, afeard the nurses will put him out. *Wake up, wee girl,* he says, *will you not wake up?*

Return

Sunday morning. He doesn't dare bring the news home. Bertie is standing at the end of the lane on the Drumagarner Road, looking out for him. 'Drive on,' he says to Jimmy Begley, staring ahead. In Kilrea he goes straight to the Rectory. Then to Cromie's and makes the arrangements – glass hearse, black horses. Travels with them in the van to Magherafelt to bring Kathleen back.

'Stop here,' he says, as they pass McIldowney's on the way home.

'You'll not get a drink today,' Cromie says, thinking he'd forgotten it was a Sunday. But Peter McIldowney takes pity. Opens a quiet bottle. There's no law broken if money doesn't change hands.

It's after midnight when they get Kathleen home. His wife won't look at him. Cromie and his lad carry the coffin into the girls' bedroom. Mrs Agnew wets the tea, coaxes the sleepless children to eat slivers of fadge. Rosie Diamond helps wash Kathleen and dress her, as she had the day she was born.

White #2

A small, plain cross. White marble. No money for a grave-surround. The soil is bare as a fresh-ploughed field.

A wagon of white stones came down from Macfin Junction. The boys in his gang looked away as he helped myself to two bucketfuls. He edged the grave with them.

The second spring there were snowdrops. It wasn't him that planted them. He rooted them out.

Each year, when the winter's back is broke, he tends her grave. Washes the stones. Scrubs away the moss and dirt. Lays them back in place. There's none but him will notice. Her mother won't leave the house.

He remembers the day he came back from France. He stood on deck and gawped at the sight of England, the white cliffs glaring in the winter light.

Homeplace

I take a wrong turning and we find ourselves in the laneway of a farmhouse Dad doesn't recognise. The lane is so narrow I've no choice but to reverse back out into the Drumagarner Road. It's a nail-biting experience. The local drivers are unforgiving of motorists who don't know where they're going. They whip out of Kilrea in their vans and 4x4s with little regard for incompetent visitors trying to reverse out of laneways. At last there's a lull in the traffic and we get back on the road. It's only another twenty or thirty yards until we get to the lane we were aiming for, tucked alongside the entrance to a local engineering company.

I'd had fears for my car axle. A few years ago one of my cousins had abandoned an attempt to visit the old homeplace because of the state of the lane, but it must have had some work done since then, because now it's covered in a thick layer of slate chippings that crackle as we drive over them. I take it slowly. My axle might be safe, but loose chippings won't do the paintwork any good. We pass a turn-off to the left where a picture-book white cottage sits. There are, literally, roses round the door. The rural charm is only slightly diminished by the warehouse of the engineering company looming in the background. 'That was Rosie Diamond's cottage,' Dad says. Rosie was the local woman called upon to deliver babies and lay out the dead. The cottage belongs to the family who own the engineering company. Nobody lives there now, but Dad showed me a story in one of the local newspapers a few months ago, recounting how the cottage had been restored by the owners and furnished with vintage fixtures and fittings.

We continue up the lane. The land to either side is the rough, unprofitable bog land known in this part of the world as 'the moss'. After another quarter mile we enter a stretch shaded by trees. 'I think it's here somewhere,' Dad says, gesturing to the right. The lane widens and I pull in. Still in the car, I peer into a tangle of willow trees. I can just make out a shape that's familiar to me from the one old photograph of the gatehouse. This is the house where my dad and his ten brothers and sisters were born.

Drumagarner gatehouse belonged to the London Midland and Scottish Railway, and was one of a series of gatehouses dotted along the thirty-odd miles of the Derry Central railway line. At key spots where the railway track crossed a road or lane there was a gatehouse. My grandparents moved into the house in the early 1920s after my grandfather started working for the LMS. I suppose getting free accommodation would have been considered a major perk of the job. The gatehouse was a single-storey dwelling with an outer shell of corrugated tin. The walls were thin, and the plastered interior was often slippery with damp. There were three small rooms – the middle one with a hearth – and a porch that served as a kitchen of sorts, although all the cooking was done over the open fire. There was a tiny window in the porch so that my grandmother could keep an eye on the railway line as she peeled potatoes or washed the dishes. Water was fetched from a spring at the edge of a nearby field, and of course there was no electricity. Both my grandfather and grandmother had grown up in farming families, in the type of thatched dwellings that look so charming to us now. In the very earliest days of their marriage they lived in a solid Victorian terrace in Magherafelt. I wonder what they made of the compact, insubstantial gatehouse?

The place was abandoned in the 1980s when its last tenant, an elderly bachelor, died. As is the way in country areas the building was not demolished but simply left to its own devices. Today, Dad and I make our careful way over the rough ground to see what's left of it. Surprisingly, given that it was such a gimcrack structure, it's pretty much intact. There are shards of broken glass in the window frames and the front door has gone. 'We had to take the door off once to carry Tommy Moore's body home,' Dad recalls. Tommy Moore had one of the small farms that lay further up the lane. His sons farmed the land while he held down a job as a train driver with the LMS. He'd walk home from work each evening along the track, carrying a lantern if it was dark. His wife would watch from the farmhouse, and when she saw the light of his lantern she knew it was time to get the food on the table. One winter evening she watched in vain, and when it became late enough for annoyance to become anxiety she sent her sons down the lane to the gatehouse. My grandfather and the Moore boys set off along the railway track towards Kilrea, and found Tommy lying on the line. He was dead – of a heart attack, the doctor later said. The problem now was how to get the body moved, which is where the door of the gatehouse came in. The menfolk retraced their steps, took the door off its hinges and used it as a makeshift stretcher to bear the body home. My grandfather's experience on the Western Front meant he knew all about the practicalities of carting bodies across difficult terrain.

*

Dad and I get closer to the gatehouse. A tree has taken root close to one of the windows, and we have to manoeuvre round it to peer inside. The floor sags like wet cardboard, revealing layers of decomposing linoleum. A collapsed bed frame lies in the corner. 'There used to be two big beds in each bedroom', he says. 'You could fit three people in the beds. My father and us boys slept in one room, and my mother and the girls in the other.' Looking now at the tiny room I can see that once those two beds were in there wouldn't have been space for much else in the way of furniture. 'My mother and father never slept in the same bed,' Dad continues. 'But I suppose they must have got together sometimes, given that they produced eleven of us.'

What with the state of the floor we decide it's not safe to go inside the gatehouse. Dad finds a loose section of window frame and starts to prise it off. I ask him what he's up to. 'A souvenir of the ancestral home,' he says. 'I'll paint it with white emulsion and mount it on a bit of board.' Dad has a fixation about creating these kinds of mementoes. He loves putting plaques on things.

In 1948 the family left the gatehouse. After the war, public housing was built in Kilrea, on land off the Lisnagrot Road, and they were given a tenancy in one of the new houses. Compared to the gatehouse it was a palace. It had a front and back parlour, a kitchen, and upstairs there were four bedrooms and a bathroom. The eldest boy, Bertie, was away and married, and three of the older children, including Dad, were working, so the family was more prosperous than it had ever been. There was money enough to buy new furniture for the house – a sofa and easy chairs, a sideboard and china cabinet. For the first time in her life my granny would have a cooker. As they prepared to leave the gatehouse they brought out all the bits of pine furniture and every other remnant of their old life. They built it into a pile and set a match to it, then stood and watched it burn until there was nothing left but ashes.

Hannah

7th June 1900 – 25th January 1983

Sounding Hill

My father's land runs to the edge of the quarry, the farmhouse tucked into a dip between hill and hill. Out of sight, but not out of sound. The siren's wail to warn of a blast. The thunderclap of dynamite. The cattle are unconcerned. They grow used to it as they turn in their mothers' bellies. I suppose I must have learned the same lesson. The noise has never startled me.

Sometimes, when I'm sent on a chore, I slip away to the high field, push through the gap in the hedge and walk to the quarry's edge. Far below the men work. The clang of sledgehammers echoes from rock-face to rock-face. Shovels rasp as the carts are loaded.

I pity the naked stone. It has slept underground since the days of creation, swaddled by the soil's soft blanketing. Now it is split, stripped, its delicate greys and greens displayed. Its immensity broken down into smaller and smaller pieces.

Quarrying is a brutal trade compared with farming. The plough turns the earth like a comb through hair, untangling it, making it prosper.

Salisbury Plain, 1917

I got word today that my father is dead and buried. I felt so far from home. Mrs Barry made me a cup of tea. Told me I could take the day off if I wished. I said I'd rather get on.

The artillery are on exercises out on the plain. The scullery windows rattle. Mr Barry is busy in the stables. There's a young stallion needs kept on a short tether. He isn't used to the gunfire yet. Mr Barry's not sure he's suited.

We travelled through London on the way here. It was nighttime. Mrs Barry let me sit in the window seat of the omnibus. The buildings gleamed in the darkness, great cliffs of pale stone. Mr Barry said we were passing Buckingham Palace. Write home to your father, he said, and tell him you've seen where the King lives.

Sea-bathing - Portstewart, 1920

When the breakfast shift is over we cross the road from the hotel to the shore. The breeze clears my head of the kitchen's heat. My borrowed bathing suit, cold with a winter's worth of damp. A housecoat, worn for decency. Someone else's sandals. I turn my ankle on the shingle.

One of the Ballymoney girls is loud and lively, running into the waves with a squeal.

I pick my way in carefully, avoiding the flurries of seaweed below the surface. My legs look so white. My arms are freckled with little scalds from spits of bacon fat.

Deeper, deeper. Up to my thighs, and the waves, when they come, rush past my waist. The tug of the current as the sea pulls back. They say someone is drowned every year.

I turn and look across the road to the hotel. Our rooms are at the back. No sea view for the kitchen girls. I duck down so that my shoulders are covered and watch the waves curl. The dark blue of their rearing up. Their tumble into foam.

Husband

Once, before we were courting, I saw him on a Saturday afternoon coming out of Pat Murray's bar. As the door swung I looked for a moment into its mysteries. The glint of bottles on the back shelf. The haze of tobacco smoke. A dim-lit kingdom of men. He scowled, looked away, pretended he hadn't seen me.

I liked him better on Sundays, all spruce for churchgoing. Boots gleaming like coal, white spats, watch-chain looped from his waistcoat buttonhole to his pocket.

He spoke about where he was reared. How he'd like some land again.

My mother told me policemen were notorious for the drink. But he said the pay was steady, and there'd be a pension if he was killed or maimed.

Sometimes he disappeared for days on end. We quarreled about it once when we were still walking out, and I didn't see him for a month. I thought that was the end of us. Feared the nudges and whispers of the other girls. I laid aside the notions I'd had – a wee house, and me setting the table for just the two of us. My sister said she'd heard he'd been posted to the station at Claudy.

Every day there was word of ambushes and riots, executions and assassinations.

And then he was at the door, dressed in his best, his face scrubbed fresh. And only because I was tired from waiting I said to my mother that, yes, she could let him in.

Gatehouse

We are folded away here, hidden where the train line pleats the land. We live at a still point, a crossing place of rail, and lane, and the path across the moss where the grey crows meet.

Turf glows in the hearth. Cheese sweats on the pantry shelf. Milk settles in its pail. I dip a finger in the cream and savour the thick taste of it.

We pray together at bedtime. He is gentle, at times, in the darkness.

Bedding

When my husband was in the police he was given a new greatcoat every winter. By the time he'd resigned in a strunce with the sergeant we had a collection of them. We brought them with us to the gatehouse to blanket the beds. They're dense black woollen weave, heavy enough to pin the wee ones down for the night.

I save cotton flour sacks, wash and bleach them, unpick the seams and fashion them into sheets and bolster cases. At night I dream of soda bread warming on the griddle.

Waiting Up

Kathleen said she would be late. Mr Kenning had asked them to stay. Bertie was home by six. Ate his praties mashed up with an egg cracked into them. I put a damp cloth over the pot, to stop the praties drying out.

Doreen helped me get the wee ones ready for bed. Hands and faces washed. Prayers said. Tucked in.

Past eight, I put a plate near the fire to warm. Moved the lamp closer to the window. Hooked the kettle on the crane to boil.

Near nine. Bertie lit a lantern and went down the lane to meet her.

Near ten. Her father said, 'They'd better pay her for the extra hours.' He took his notebook from his pocket. Licked the pencil. Wrote.

I thought to myself, *Kathleen said she would be late.*

Into Darkness

I sit up late, to keep away from him. This house is full of breath. Nine hearts a-beating.

I pretend I am back at Sounding Hill, a child again, my belly neat, unripe, untroubled. The siren wails. The dynamite explodes and I am blown apart, the raw rock gaping where my life was.

If love is a prayer it goes unheard.

He's rarely in the house. Takes extra hours at work. Sometimes comes home trailing the smell of drink. I cannot look at him.

There's a woman in Moneydig lost her wits and knelt down in the train's path. I overheard Bertie talking about it with Lily Agnew. I'm not supposed to know.

Seam

A meeting of fabric. A line of junction. A suture. A crack.

The mark of a cut. A furrow planted with pain. A hidden thing, dark and precious held fast inside a family. Secrets are stitched in the seams. Corrosive threads. You on the drink. Words we will not speak.

A wound too deep.

Wee Late One

Rosaline was born nearly two years to the day after Kathleen left us. I thought I was finished with babies then, me being the age I was. But three years later along came Eileen. The house was crowded with my husband's moods. Bertie had married Bellingham's daughter. Our girls were restless, and the wee ones crabbit. I couldn't get peace to cry.

There was a wild lot of sickness that winter. War weariness, some said. When Eileen took bad I felt that dread on me. She couldn't get a breath.

'There's new medicine,' Dr Boyd said. The tablets were near the size of a broad bean. M&Bs, he called them. 'Grind them up into powder,' he said, 'and mix it in with her milk.'

I did as he telled me. Coaxed it into her on a teaspoon, three times a day. In between times she gurned and slept. Rosie Diamond shook her head. 'I don't think she'll do,' she said.

And then, a week in, Eileen stirred in her crib. I went over to look. She smiled up at me. Her first smile.

The house was empty, for once. There was no one to tell. So I sat and watched her sleep, counting her easy breaths.

Dressmaking

It's November 2017. Three and a half metres of ivory linen fabric lie spread along the hall floor, folded lengthways in preparation for cutting. The six pieces of the dressmaking pattern are held in place with flat stones. The tissue-paper pattern is over seventy years old and so fragile with age that I daren't stick pins in it. The linen is from William Clark & Sons, and it cost me nearly £70 a metre. I lift my fabric scissors and gather the courage to make the first cut. My anxiety isn't simply because the fabric is expensive, it's more what this first cut represents. This is the moment when I truly commit to a creative project unlike any other I've engaged in before: making a dress that will tell Kathleen's story.

This moment has been several years in the making, starting long before I began to think of writing about Kathleen. I've dabbled in textile crafts since my late teens, with short-lived but recurrent bursts of enthusiasm for embroidery, knitting and dressmaking. My most recent ventures have been in crochet and hand-spinning.

Ironically I'd taken up these latest crafts as a counterbalance to my work as a writer, never thinking that working in textiles could become a way of 'writing' – or of telling a story at any rate. Writing is a strangely disembodied activity – the physically effortless tapping on the keyboard, the long hours spent inside one's own mind. Even the end product, in these days of ebooks and online publishing, often has no physical form. Textile craft speaks to the human need to make – even if in my case all I made were a few skeins of lumpy yarn and more shapeless crocheted hats than a person could ever want.

However, as I thought about Kathleen the idea slowly took hold that actually making something – an artefact rather than a text – might tell her story more fittingly than words could. Writing happens in two dimensions – it's literally flat – whereas a textile artefact such as a dress is three dimensional, and echoes the contours of the human body it is designed to adorn. So I decided I would tell her story in the form of a linen dress. I couldn't bring myself to leave words behind entirely, but instead of writing them down on the page I would embroider them onto the fabric. The dress would be my gift to her, a way of honouring the short time she had, and mourning the many years she never saw. I imagined a different future for her, one where her supervisor had let her leave work fifteen minutes earlier or made her stay ten minutes later that damp December evening in 1939. Or where the farmer walking the road had been delayed in Upperlands for another half an hour. A future where that quiet, disastrous collision at the Cross Keys had never happened, and Kathleen had cycled on safely back to the tiny, crowded gatehouse and a table piled high with praties fresh from the pot. In that future she'd have celebrated her twenty-first birthday by having a dress made by Tillie Moore the dressmaker. It would not have been extravagant – simple cotton, no doubt, but pretty enough to wear to a dance. And that is how my first real venture into textile art began.

I found a dressmaking pattern from the mid-1940s for sale on eBay. It arrived in a disintegrating outer envelope, illustrated with line drawings of a trim young woman wearing three different configurations of the simple, button-through pattern: frock, housecoat and beach coat.

Every element of it spoke of wartime frugality when everything was rationed. The instructions were tightly printed on a sheet of paper about the size of a foolscap page. Unlike modern dressmaking patterns, the tissue paper pattern pieces were unprinted – presumably to save ink – and the letters identifying them had been added with a hole-punch, as had the marks for darts and other details of fit and assembly. Some earlier owner had helpfully written the piece names on in pencil: bodice back, skirt back. The design itself – like that of most mid-40s attire – worked on the principle of minimising the amount of fabric needed. There were no frills or gathers, no wasteful fullness in the line or silhouette.

It was a stroke of luck that I'd been able to source my linen from William Clark & Sons. Unlike many textile manufacturers in this part of the world the firm has survived the seismic changes that have decimated domestic textile production over the last number of decades. Sadly, though, the era when fine dress linens are woven in Upperlands is long past. Clark's now specialise in 'finishing' linen, which means they take untreated linen cloth and subject it to various processes such as dying, beetling and shrinking that make it useable for high-end curtains, cushions and upholstery. Upholstery linen is typically made with heavier threads than dress linen and is more loosely woven. That makes it stiff, and not the sort of material you'd normally use for a garment. Nonetheless, it felt right that Kathleen's dress should be made from linen that came from the very place she'd worked. William Clark & Sons don't normally sell directly to the public, but the Creative Director, Duncan Neil, listened sympathetically to my explanation when I arrived unannounced at the factory one day with my father in tow. Duncan helped me choose a plain ivory linen: its simplicity and innocence seemed fitting for the young girl Kathleen had been, and always would be.

Before cutting into my precious linen I had made a practice version of the dress in gauzy muslin. This is known in dressmaking as a *toile*, from the French word for 'tissue'. The purpose of the *toile* is usually to check for fit – it's a trial-run garment made with cheap fabric. In my case I was sewing it to refresh my rusty dressmaking skills, and make the construction mistakes I didn't dare make once I was working on the linen. I later found out that choosing muslin for my *toile* was based on a misunderstanding. I hadn't realised that in the world of dressmaking 'muslin' is simply another term for a *toile*. The trial garment should actually be made out of cotton calico, a robust, no-nonsense fabric much better suited to the purpose than loose-woven, muslin gauze. Nevertheless, my mistake was a happy accident, for a muslin gauze *toile* is a sad and beautiful thing, fragile and ethereal.

The time spent working on the *toile* and then the dress proper gave me time to think about how I would 'write' the story on the fabric, and what words I would use. I wanted to capture a sense of the living girl – excited to have got a start in a decent job with good prospects; proud to be contributing to the family finances; wondering and worrying what the war would mean; dreaming of a future with dances and new clothes. I wanted my imagined Kathleen to be alert to the world around her – its smells and colours and tastes. So I began to write fictional fragments, imagining Kathleen's journey to and from work that summer of 1939. I unearthed Clark's order books at the Public Record Office of Northern Ireland – enormous ledgers that had to be wheeled to me on a trolley – and learnt the arcane terminology of the linen trade: black buckram, slate Holland, shrunk duck, dove pocketing, bleached mercerised linen suiting. The pages from December 1939 are full of orders for blackout cloth. The military convalescent depot at the New Savoy Hotel in Bangor wants 700 yards, Palace Barracks in Holywood wants 500 yards, and St Patrick's Barracks in Ballymena wants 900 yards. Every order is prefaced with the words *At Once*. I thought about how those order books opened up new words and worlds to Kathleen, and how that might have fed her imagination.

To equip myself with the skills of writing in stitch I signed up for a residential course run by artist Rosalind Wyatt. She's a calligrapher by training, and has profound knowledge of the way handwriting is constructed. Her skill with a needle means she can replicate handwritten words in stitch, catching loops of thread with barely visible couching stitches. Her work is not simply decorative. It's about creating an intimate dialogue between words and textiles.

It would have been wonderful if I'd had an example of Kathleen's handwriting, but none exists. The only handwriting I had to work with was in an old pocket notebook belonging to my grandfather. It's 16cm x 10cm, with a dark red cover and lined pages. He used it to take note of the hours he'd worked for the LMS, and other details of his job. The first entry is 20th March 1942, just over three years after Kathleen's death. He writes in a casual copperplate, sometimes copying out individual words – *accommodation, permission* - as if to check the spelling, and he starts nearly every noun with an upper-case letter. Under Rosalind's careful tutelage I selected a few snippets that seemed to convey his personality – *I bought a pair of Waring Boots at 35 Shillings; I Bought one Pig on Friday; No. of my Bicycle RH68317* – and began to stitch them onto the sleeves of the dress. I decided to use a deep khaki coloured thread for his words, as a nod to his time in the army during the First World War.

Kathleen's words were, of course, a product of my imagination. I wrote my way in to her past and present: her memories of the death of her baby sister; her observations on her father's character; her modest dreams for the future. To stitch her words I chose a thread that was as close as I could find to the blue of the flax flower. I wrote the fragments out by hand, doing my best to change my 21st-century scrawl to something closer to the neat cursive script Kathleen would have learnt at the Mercers' School in Kilrea.

There was one more voice I wanted to give space to on the dress – Kathleen's mother, my grandmother. My memories of her were of a kindly, quiet woman, dressed always in a dark skirt and a white blouse with a brooch at the neck. She retained a beautiful complexion all her eighty-two years. On our family visits to Kilrea she would busy herself in preparing tea, sandwiches and buns, not taking anything herself until the guests were fed and watered. It was only as I worked on the dress that I really considered the sadness running through her life. She had buried two daughters. Her husband's bad moods and fixations had driven several of the surviving children away. I thought of their sixty years of marriage, and the bitterness and sorrow buried in their silences. For her I chose a thread in deep maroon, which seemed to me like a mournful colour, and stitched her words along one of the seam-lines of the dress where they would be almost unnoticed, as she had been through most of her life.

Writing in stitch is a laborious, time-consuming task. Words mean so much more to me when I write them stitch-by-stitch. They become a physical thing as well as a symbol or signifier, so that when I read a word I see both the thing it means and understand it's material presence. I'm used to rattling out words on a keyboard – I'm a trained typist, so I'm quick – and that's great for catching thoughts in flight. But sewing words brings about a different relationship with them. The dress I was stitching on became as familiar as a comfort blanket. It was in my hands every day, and I came to know how the fabric responded, how best to work with it. There was a sense of connection – communion, almost – that doesn't happen when writing with any other media.

In addition to the words, I embellished the dress with silk prints of various images: old family photographs, a picture of the gatehouse, my grandfather's army record, pages from William Clark & Sons' order book. On the back skirt of the dress I stitched a map of the district, based on an Ordnance Survey map from 1900. Finally, I appliquéd the garment with scraps of vintage floral cotton -linen fabric – the sort of fabric Kathleen might have had made into a dress.

One of the things I loved about telling a story in the form of a dress is that there was no dramatic arc. The reader can absorb in the story in their own way, choosing what to read and in whatever order they please. They might not notice some parts, or misunderstand others. There's no beginning, and no end.

When I first embarked on making Kathleen's dress I started an Instagram account to chart my progress. Over the weeks and months the account gained a modest number of followers, including stitchers and weavers, people with family connections to the linen industry, natives of Kilrea and – most significantly for the project – curators and gallerists. It was through one of these latter new connections that the dress came to be included in the 'Lost in Linen' exhibition as part of the first Linen Biennale in 2018. What had begun as personal act of remembrance and memorialisation was now part of a public conversation. There seemed to be something in the project that connected emotionally with people, and many of those I spoke to shared stories of loss and tragedy in their own families.

The whole experience brought home to me the limitations of writing as a way of telling a story. Reading is a private activity, and one that many people either do not wish to do, or feel is not really for them. *Looking*, however, is a whole other experience. As I stood in the background at the 'Lost in Linen' exhibition watching visitors examine the dress, I realised how rich the experience of looking is. People engaged with the dress, studying the stitched words and images, pointing out new discoveries to their companions. Visual art can be intimidating, but there seemed to be something about this piece – its human scale, perhaps, or the sheer domesticity of it's being recognisably a garment – that made visitors feel comfortable in 'reading' it.

Kathleen's dress is a piece of art that can be folded up and put in a carrier bag, and in this manner it has travelled with me to talks in village halls, to radio broadcasts and to conferences. I have no wish for it to be preserved in a glass case. My request to anyone who encounters it is the opposite of the usual gallery or museum instruction. Please Touch. It won't break.

Afterword

The problem with writers is that they can't stop themselves from writing, even when making a piece of textile art. I had more of Kathleen's words than I could fit on the dress. And then came Thomas and Hannah's voices, more insistent as time went on. What began as an alternative to a written story spilled over onto the page, and became the book you are reading.

At heart, though, Kathleen's story is told by the dress. It's compact and unassuming, like the young woman it was made to fit, a young woman with the slim waist and narrow back of her wartime generation. It's embellished with scraps and fragments – words, pictures, maps and absences. There are loose threads and frayed hems, because Kathleen's was an unfinished story. I once read that when a person dies young they cast a shadow across all the years they should have lived, and it's true that the pain of Kathleen's death is still felt – albeit faintly – within the family. But Kathleen's dress, Kathleen's story, is not about shadows. It's about life, in all its quiet glory.

Acknowledgements

So many people have supported A Dress for Kathleen from its inception as a piece of textile art to its evolution into this book. My special thanks to: the Arts Council of Northern Ireland, who gave generous support as the idea took shape; Maria McManus, for her unwavering passion for the project; Moyra Donaldson, for listening to my ramblings as I began to conceive the idea of the book; Róisín McPhilemy for her astute feedback on my first draft; Robert Martin at R-Space Gallery for exhibiting the dress as part of the Linen Biennale; and Sarah Bower, for suggesting I contact Story Machine with my manuscript. Thanks also to my friends in the Irish chapter of the Historical Novelists Society for their advice, and the many friends and colleagues at the Open University who have taken such an interest in the project.

Thank you for supporting planet-friendly publishing

Story Machine seeks to have a net positive social and environmental impact. That means the environment and people's lives are actually better off for every book we print. Story Machine offsets our entire carbon footprint plus 10% through a www.ClimateCare.org programme. We are now investing in converting to use only 100% renewable energies and seeking out the most planet-positive means of shipping books to our readers.

The printing industry is a huge polluter, requiring the use of huge amounts of water, toxic chemicals, and energy. Even FSC certified mix paper sources drive deforestation. That's why we are proud to be working with www.Seacort.net, a global leader in planet positive printing. Not only have they developed a waterless and chemical-free process, they use only 100% renewable energies, FSC certified recycled paper, and direct absolutely no waste to landfill. That's why they were crowned Europe's most sustainable SME in 2017, and have been recognised as one of the top three environmental printers in the world.

Planet-positive printing costs us a little more. But we think this is a small price to pay for a better world, today and in the future. If you agree, please share our message, and encourage other publishers and authors to commit to planet-positive printing. Stories can change the world. They deserve publishers that want to make sure they do. Together, we can make publishing more sustainable.